Under Training

Danica Kassebaum

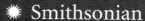 Smithsonian

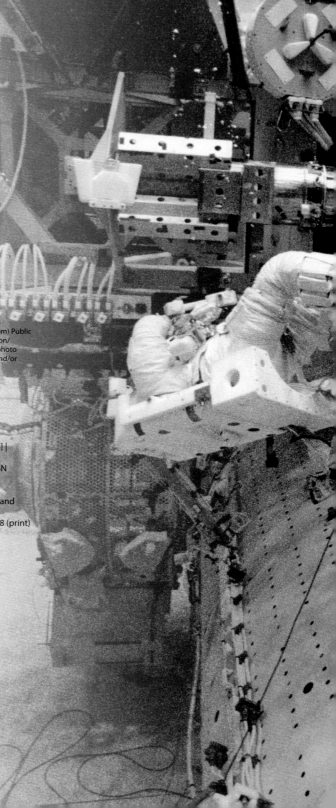

Contributing Author

Allison Duarte, M.A.

Consultants

Tamieka Grizzle, Ed.D.
K–5 STEM Lab Instructor
Harmony Leland Elementary School

Valerie Neal
Curator and Chairperson of the Space History Department
Smithsonian National Air and Space Museum

Publishing Credits

Rachelle Cracchiolo, M.S.Ed., *Publisher*
Conni Medina, M.A.Ed., *Managing Editor*
Diana Kenney, M.A.Ed., NBCT, *Content Director*
Véronique Bos, *Creative Director*
June Kikuchi, *Content Director*
Robin Erickson, *Art Director*
Seth Rogers, *Editor*
Mindy Duits, *Senior Graphic Designer*
Smithsonian Science Education Center

Image Credits: front cover, pp.2–3, pp.4–5, p.6 (insert), pp.6–7, p.7 (top), p.10, 11 (bottom), p.12, p.13, p.14, p.15, p.17 (top), p.19 (both), 32 (right) NASA; p.7 (bottom) Public Domain; p.8 Vicspacewalker/Shutterstock, pp.16–17, p.18 Stephen Frink Collection/Alamy; p.22 UpperCut Images/Alamy; p.24 FDR Presidential Library & Museum, photo by Margaret Suckley; p.27 (top) Aabejon/Getty Images; all other images iStock and/or Shutterstock.

Library of Congress Cataloging-in-Publication Data

Names: Kassebaum, Danica, author.
Title: Underwater training / Danica Kassebaum.
Description: Huntington Beach, CA : Teacher Created Materials, [2018] | Audience: K to grade 3. | Includes index.
Identifiers: LCCN 2017060490 (print) | LCCN 2017061607 (ebook) | ISBN 9781493869220 (e-book) | ISBN 9781493866823 (pbk.)
Subjects: LCSH: Aquatic exercises--Juvenile literature. | Aquatic exercises--Therapeutic use--Juvenile literature. | Physical education and training--Juvenile literature.
Classification: LCC GV838.53.E94 (ebook) | LCC GV838.53.E94 K36 2018 (print) | DDC 613.7/16--dc23
LC record available at https://lccn.loc.gov/2017060490

Smithsonian

Teacher Created Materials

5301 Oceanus Drive
Huntington Beach, CA 92649-1030
www.tcmpub.com

ISBN 978-1-4938-6682-3
© 2019 Teacher Created Materials, Inc.

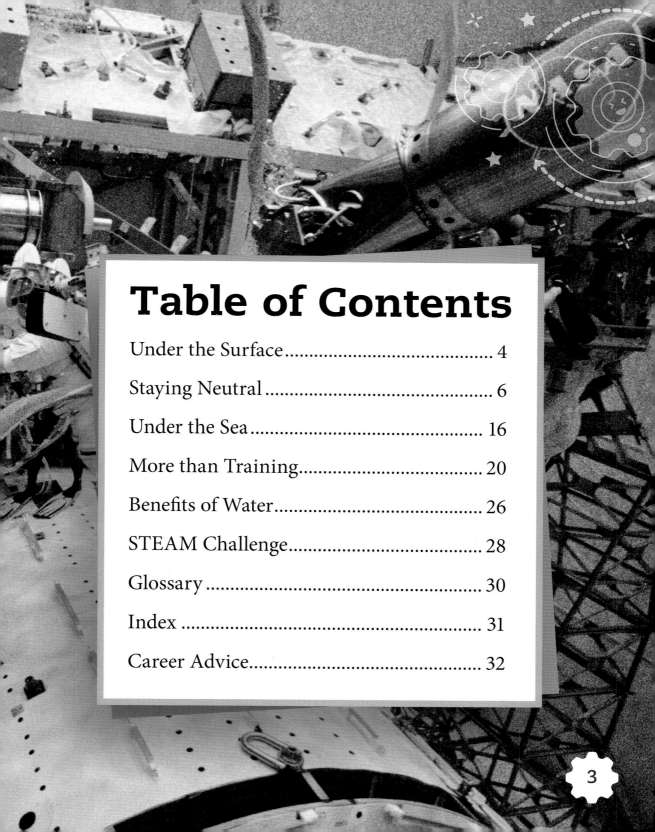

Table of Contents

Under the Surface

Water is used for many things. You drink it. You use it to wash things. You swim in it. But, did you know water is used to train **astronauts**?

There is very little **gravity** in space. That means that astronauts float around in their spacecraft. This makes them feel weightless. Training in water helps them get ready for what it feels like to be in space.

Astronauts are not the only people who train in water. Athletes train in water, too. Water can also be used to help people get better after they have been injured. And water can help people with **chronic** conditions, such as arthritis.

Astronaut Robert L. Curbeam Jr. trains in a pool.

An athlete swims in a pool.

These women exercise with weights in a pool.

Staying Neutral

You may have noticed that objects that are heavy on land seem lighter when they are in the water. This is because they are more **buoyant** in water than they are on land. That makes some things that are hard to do on land much easier in water. In the pool, you can lift your friends with ease. You can even float!

The feeling you have when you are in water is almost what it feels like to be in space. In fact, some astronauts train for space in water. They train in **labs** that have large pools. While in the pools, astronauts wear weights so that they don't float to the top or sink to the bottom. This is called *neutral buoyancy* (BOY-uhn-see).

NASA's Neutral Buoyancy Lab

An astronaut trains in a neutral buoyancy pool.

When Archimedes (ahr-kuh-MEE-deez) discovered buoyancy, he is said to have cried, "Eureka!" It means "I have found it." It is now a well-known phrase when someone figures something out.

Train Around the World

There are neutral buoyancy pools all over the world. There is one in Russia. There is also one in Germany. Chinese astronauts practice in a pool in Beijing.

In the United States, there is a pool in Houston, Texas. It was built in 1995. It is part of the Neutral Buoyancy Lab. Many things are placed in the pool to help astronauts train. Even space stations have been put in the pool! When an entire station does not fit in the pool, it is split into pieces. A big crane is used to put pieces in the pool.

Astronaut Michael Barratt trains for a space walk in a pool in Russia.

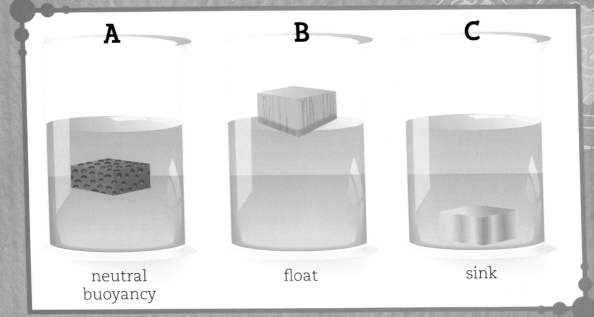

A   B   C

neutral buoyancy   float   sink

Density

To understand how underwater training works, you need to understand density. Density is the amount of **matter** in an object compared to how big it is. Things that are less dense than water will float (see B above). Objects that are more dense than water will sink (see C above). When an object has the same density as water, it will suspend in the water (see A above). It will not sink or float. This is called *neutral buoyancy*. It makes you feel almost weightless.

Practice, Practice, Practice

There is very little gravity in space. It feels different from being on Earth. A neutral buoyancy pool allows astronauts to get used to this feeling. It makes them feel as though they are in space. Astronauts spend many hours in neutral buoyancy pools. They practice what they will do in space. Anything that is going to be done in space must be done in the water first. They practice how to move in space. They practice how to fix parts of the space station, such as **telescopes**.

NASA astronauts practice for a mission in space at the Neutral Buoyancy Lab.

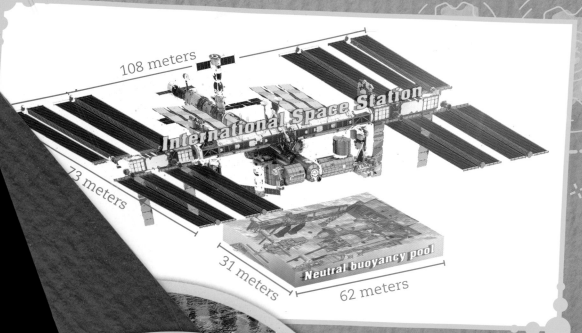

108 meters

International Space Station

73 meters

Neutral buoyancy pool

31 meters

62 meters

Pool

buoyancy pool in Houston
meters (202 feet) long
wide. It is 12 m (40 ft.)
ds over 23 million liters
water! Parts of the
tion (ISS) have
tral Buoyancy
SS is much
nt sections are
are in space.

Working in space is very different from working on Earth. If you drop something in space, you cannot just pick it up. It will float away. It is hard to get new supplies into space. So, if a tool is lost, it can be hard to replace. Astronauts need to be ready before they travel to space. They practice a lot on Earth before they board the shuttle. This lessens the chance of losing or dropping things in space.

Working underwater is not quite the same as working in space. You do not experience the same weightless feeling. In a pool, you can feel your weight. There is also fluid resistance. It is more difficult to move your limbs. The water creates resistance that space does not. But these special pools are the best way to prepare for space.

An astronaut practices using tools she will use in space.

An astronaut trains for a mission at the Neutral Buoyancy Lab while divers watch and assist.

Natatorium (nay-tuh-TOHR-ee-uhm) is another word for *indoor pool*. It is a pool that is in its own building.

What to Wear?

When astronauts are in neutral buoyancy pools, they wear special space suits. The suits are a lot like what they wear in space. But, most of the electronics have been taken out. The suits have special weights in them. The weights keep the wearer neutrally buoyant. They do not sink to the bottom of the pool. They also do not float to the top.

Working in the suits is not easy. They are very stiff. Astronauts have to practice moving in these suits. They have to move differently than they would on Earth. Wearing these special suits in the water helps astronauts feel what it will be like when they are in space.

Two astronauts are lowered into the pool with a crane.

An astronaut puts on his space suit.

Out-of-This-World Fashion

Space suits are designed to be functional. They help astronauts breathe and stay safe. They have many different parts and layers. But designers want suits to look nice, too. When people think of space travel, they picture space suits. The suits are a symbol of the space program. Designers spend time choosing colors, adding details, and making the suits as comfortable as possible.

Under the Sea

   Astronauts often spend many days in space. They live on a space shuttle or a space station. Life in space is very different from life on land. To help them get ready, some go live in the ocean.

   There is a lab deep in the ocean off the coast of Florida where some astronauts go to train. The lab is called Aquarius. It is the size of a school bus. A space station is about the same size.

   Astronauts can spend many days living in the lab. Up to seven astronauts at a time can stay there. This helps them get used to living together in a small area. While they are at Aquarius, they do research. They go outside the lab to practice working in space. All of this gets them ready for life in space.

Aquarius

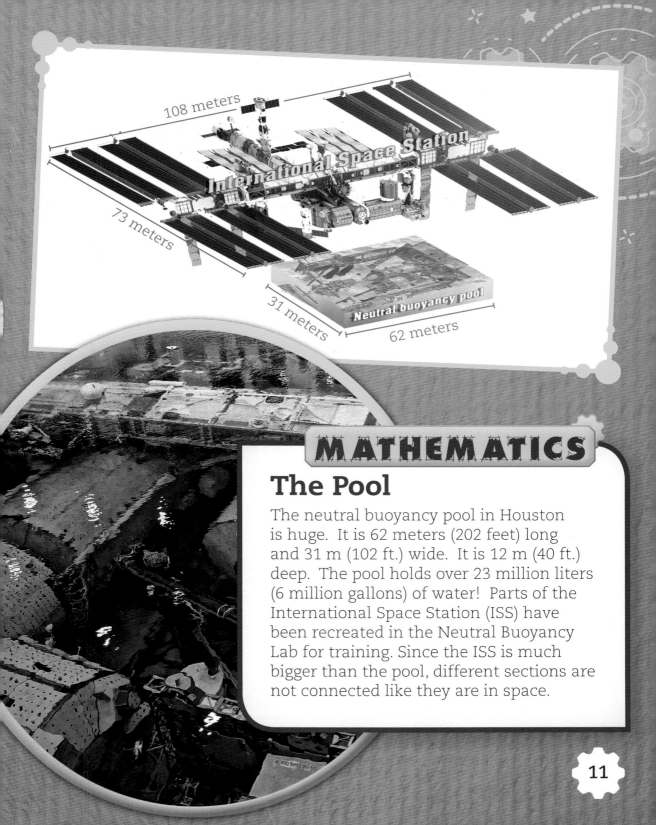

108 meters

International Space Station

73 meters

31 meters

62 meters

Neutral buoyancy pool

MATHEMATICS

The Pool

The neutral buoyancy pool in Houston is huge. It is 62 meters (202 feet) long and 31 m (102 ft.) wide. It is 12 m (40 ft.) deep. The pool holds over 23 million liters (6 million gallons) of water! Parts of the International Space Station (ISS) have been recreated in the Neutral Buoyancy Lab for training. Since the ISS is much bigger than the pool, different sections are not connected like they are in space.

Working in space is very different from working on Earth. If you drop something in space, you cannot just pick it up. It will float away. It is hard to get new supplies into space. So, if a tool is lost, it can be hard to replace. Astronauts need to be ready before they travel to space. They practice a lot on Earth before they board the shuttle. This lessens the chance of losing or dropping things in space.

Working underwater is not quite the same as working in space. You do not experience the same weightless feeling. In a pool, you can feel your weight. There is also fluid resistance. It is more difficult to move your limbs. The water creates resistance that space does not. But these special pools are the best way to prepare for space.

An astronaut practices using tools she will use in space.

An astronaut trains for a mission at the Neutr[al] Buoyancy Lab while di[vers] watch and assist.

Natatorium (nay-tuh-TOHR-ee-uhm) is another word for *indoor pool*. It is a pool that is in its own building.

What to Wear?

When astronauts are in neutral buoyancy pools, they wear special space suits. The suits are a lot like what they wear in space. But, most of the electronics have been taken out. The suits have special weights in them. The weights keep the wearer neutrally buoyant. They do not sink to the bottom of the pool. They also do not float to the top.

Working in the suits is not easy. They are very stiff. Astronauts have to practice moving in these suits. They have to move differently than they would on Earth. Wearing these special suits in the water helps astronauts feel what it will be like when they are in space.

Two astronauts are lowered into the pool with a crane.

An astronaut puts on his space suit.

Out-of-This-World Fashion

Space suits are designed to be functional. They help astronauts breathe and stay safe. They have many different parts and layers. But designers want suits to look nice, too. When people think of space travel, they picture space suits. The suits are a symbol of the space program. Designers spend time choosing colors, adding details, and making the suits as comfortable as possible.

Under the Sea

Astronauts often spend many days in space. They live on a space shuttle or a space station. Life in space is very different from life on land. To help them get ready, some go live in the ocean.

There is a lab deep in the ocean off the coast of Florida where some astronauts go to train. The lab is called Aquarius. It is the size of a school bus. A space station is about the same size.

Astronauts can spend many days living in the lab. Up to seven astronauts at a time can stay there. This helps them get used to living together in a small area. While they are at Aquarius, they do research. They go outside the lab to practice working in space. All of this gets them ready for life in space.

Aquarius

Two scientists work inside Aquarius.

ENGINEERING

Strong as Steel

Aquarius was built to survive large storms and hurricanes. It weighs 73 metric tons (81 tons) and is 13 m (43 ft.) long. It sits on top of a base that weighs 109 metric tons (120 tons). There are four legs on the base. The legs can move up to 2 m (7 ft.) to adjust for movement of the seafloor.

Other scientists use the underwater lab, too. **Engineers** go to the lab to study the coral reef. They also study the ocean. They learn a lot while they live and work under the water.

Most missions at Aquarius last around two weeks. Divers can be in the water for six to nine hours each day. This gives them time to explore and test equipment. When they dive from land, they can only spend a few hours in the water each day. They can get sick if they stay longer. The change in pressure is hard on their bodies.

Astronauts train outside of Aquarius.

International astronauts pose at Aquarius.

Astronauts who have been to Aquarius and into space have a special name. They are called *aquastronauts* (uh-KWAH-struh-nots).

A NASA astronaut works with tools underwater.

More than Training

You don't have to be an astronaut to train in water. Athletes work out in pools. It helps them build strength.

Work It Out

Water exercises are a great way to train. You can exercise in a pool. You can even exercise in a special tank of water. In water, there is less pressure on your body. Some movements that are hard on land are easy in water. For example, many people can't do a handstand on land. But, in a pool, it is much easier to hold yourself up with your arms. This is because of the buoyancy of water. It makes you feel almost weightless. Water is also good for weak muscles. Try running in a pool. It is much harder than it is to run on land. Water creates a natural resistance that can build muscles.

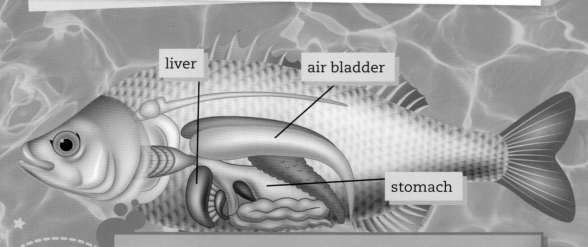

liver

air bladder

stomach

Most fish can control their buoyancy. They have air in their bodies to help them suspend in water. The extra air is stored in an organ called an air bladder.

People use foam weights and water resistance to build their muscles.

A woman exercises in water.

Injuries

Water can help when you hurt a muscle or a bone. Because of buoyancy, people who are injured can do more exercise in water than they can on land. Injured athletes can stay in shape while they heal. There is less **stress** on their bodies when they train in water. **Physical therapists** often take injured athletes to pools to help them get back in shape.

The temperature of the water makes a difference. Warm water relaxes muscles. Cold water stops muscles from swelling. Therapists choose which is best for their patients.

This physical therapist works with a patient.

TECHNOLOGY

Running Underwater

Underwater treadmills can be used to help people recover from injuries. Running on an underwater treadmill puts less stress on a person's body. Some underwater treadmills may even have cameras so physical therapists can make sure patients are walking or running correctly.

Many different exercises can be done in the water.

Chronic Problems

Water can be used to help people with chronic conditions. Sometimes, these long-lasting conditions cause pain. Doing exercises in the water can help to ease the pain.

Some people who have chronic pain use a special device called a float tank. The tank is filled with water and Epsom salt. The salt makes the water denser. This makes the person in the tank float to the top. The water is kept at body temperature, so it doesn't feel warm or cold to the touch.

Inside, a float tank is silent. It is completely dark. The water makes the person in the tank feel like they are weightless. There is very little strain on muscles and joints. This helps ease chronic pain.

Franklin D. Roosevelt was the 32nd U.S. president. He had a disease called **polio**. He used water treatments to reduce his chronic pain.

A woman relaxes
in a float tank.

float tank

Benefits of Water

Astronauts train in water. Athletes do, too. People work out in pools to recover from injuries. People with chronic pain often have less pain by moving in water. Why do so many people use pools to train and get better?

Scientists and doctors know that water is helpful. Physical therapists know this, too. They watch how people move in water. Then, they come up with ways to help. They might design better space suits. They might think of new exercises.

The next time you are in a pool, think about all the ways pools can be used. They are not just for swimming!

These people train in a pool.

STEAM CHALLENGE

Define the Problem

An important part of astronaut training happens right here on Earth! Scientists have asked you to make a neutrally buoyant underwater lab. Can you change an object to make it neutrally buoyant?

Constraints: You can only use three types of materials to make the object.

Criteria: The object must stay neutrally buoyant in a water tank for 30 seconds.

Research and Brainstorm

How does training in water prepare astronauts for space? What does it mean to be neutrally buoyant? What could you add to an object that floats to make it sink?

Design and Build

Observe the materials. Then, sketch your design of the object. What purpose will each part serve? What materials will work best? Build the model.

Test and Improve

Test your object in the water tank. Did it work? How can you improve it? Modify your design by adding to it or removing from it. Try it again.

Reflect and Share

Do you think the object would be neutrally buoyant in other types of liquid? What about this challenge was most difficult? How did you overcome it?

Glossary

astronauts—people who go to space

buoyant—able to float

chronic—something that continues for a long time or returns often

engineers—people who design and build complex products, systems, machines, or structures

fluid resistance—the opposing or slowing force of liquid

gravity—a force that acts between objects, pulling one toward the other

labs—places used for science experiments

matter—what everything is made up of

physical therapists—people who treat injuries, sometimes using water or heat

polio—a serious illness that can make a person unable to move

stress—force or pressure

telescopes—devices that use lenses to make objects appear closer and larger